On Chinese New Year

El Año Nuevo Chino

written by **Judy Zocchi**

illustrated by **Rebecca Wallis**

dingles&company New Jersey

First printing

PUBLISHED BY dingles&company

P.O. Box 508 • Sea Girt, New Jersey • 08750

WEBSITE: www.dingles.com • E-MAIL: info@dingles.com

Library of Congress Catalog Card No.: 2004091740
ISBN: 1-891997-56-4

Printed in the United States of America

For Mary and Frankie

ART DIRECTION & DESIGN Barbie Lambert
ENGLISH EDITED BY Andrea Curley
SPANISH EDITED BY Teresa Carbajal Ravet
RESEARCH AND ADDITIONAL COPY WRITTEN BY Robert Neal Kanner
EDUCATIONAL CONSULTANT Anita Tarquinio-Marcocci
CRAFT CREATED BY the Aldorasi family
PHOTOGRAPHY BY Sara Sagliano
PRE-PRESS BY Pixel Graphics

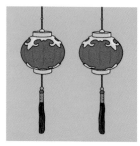
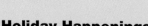

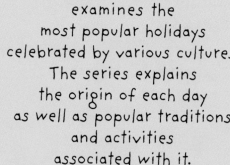
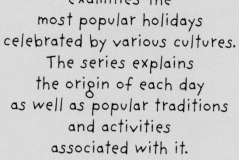

Holiday Happenings

examines the
most popular holidays
celebrated by various cultures.
The series explains
the origin of each day
as well as popular traditions
and activities
associated with it.

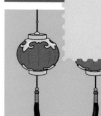

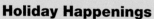

On Chinese New Year you might decorate your freshly cleaned house

Durante el Año Nuevo Chino puedes decorar tu casa recién limpia

Chinese families decorate their homes with flowers that blossom at the time of the New Year. These flowers represent rebirth and new growth for the coming year. Families also hang red scrolls or banners with expressions of good wishes on doors and walls.

with fresh flowers and scrolls.

con flores frescas y rollos de pergamino.

Las familias chinas decoran sus casas con flores que florecen al mismo tiempo del Año Nuevo. Estas flores representan el renacimiento y nuevo desarrollo para el año entrante. Las familias también cuelgan rollos rojos de pergamino o estandartes con expresiones de deseos de felicidad en las puertas y las paredes.

Then you put out
some sweets
in your prettiest bowls!

¡Luego colocas
algunas golosinas
en tus dulceras bonitas!

On Chinese New Year you might put on new clothes

Durante el Año Nuevo Chino puedes vestirte en ropa nueva

and buy some oranges to give away.

y comprar algunas naranjas para regalar.

Then you go visiting
friends and family
all day.

Luego visitas
a tus amigos y familia
todo el día.

Parents, grandparents, and close neighbors usually give children and young adults red packets containing money to symbolize the giving of good fortune. In China red is regarded as the lucky color.

On Chinese New Year you might receive a red envelope

Durante el Año Nuevo Chino puedes recibir un sobre rojo

Usualmente padres, abuelos, y vecinos entrañables les dan sobres rojos con dinero a los niños y jóvenes para simbolizar el regalo de buenaventura. En la China el color rojo se considera como color de buena suerte.

Special foods are prepared for the holiday. Most dishes that are served have symbolic meanings: whole chicken and whole fish represent togetherness and prosperity, noodles represent longevity, and sweet steamed rice cakes symbolize a rich, sweet life.

and sit down with your family for a feast.

y sentarte con tu familia para un festín.

Comidas especiales se preparan para la festividad. Muchos platos que se sirven tienen significación simbólica: el pollo entero y el pescado entero representan la unidad y la prosperidad, fideos representan una larga vida, y tortas de arroz dulce a vapor simbolizan una vida rica y dulce.

Then you honor
your ancestors
who are deceased.

Luego reconoces
a tus antepasados
muertos.

The Lantern Festival occurs on the day
of the first full moon of the New Year. The day's
most important activity is looking at lanterns. Decorated
lanterns are hung everywhere, and people carry
them to an evening parade under the light
of the full moon.

On Chinese New Year
you might hang out a lantern

Durante el Año Nuevo Chino
puedes colgar una linterna

El Festival de la Linterna ocurre el día
de la primera luna llena del Año Nuevo. La actividad más
importante del día es mirar las linternas. Linternas decoradas
se cuelgan por donde quiera, y la gente carga con ellas
durante el desfile de la noche bajo la
luz de la luna llena.

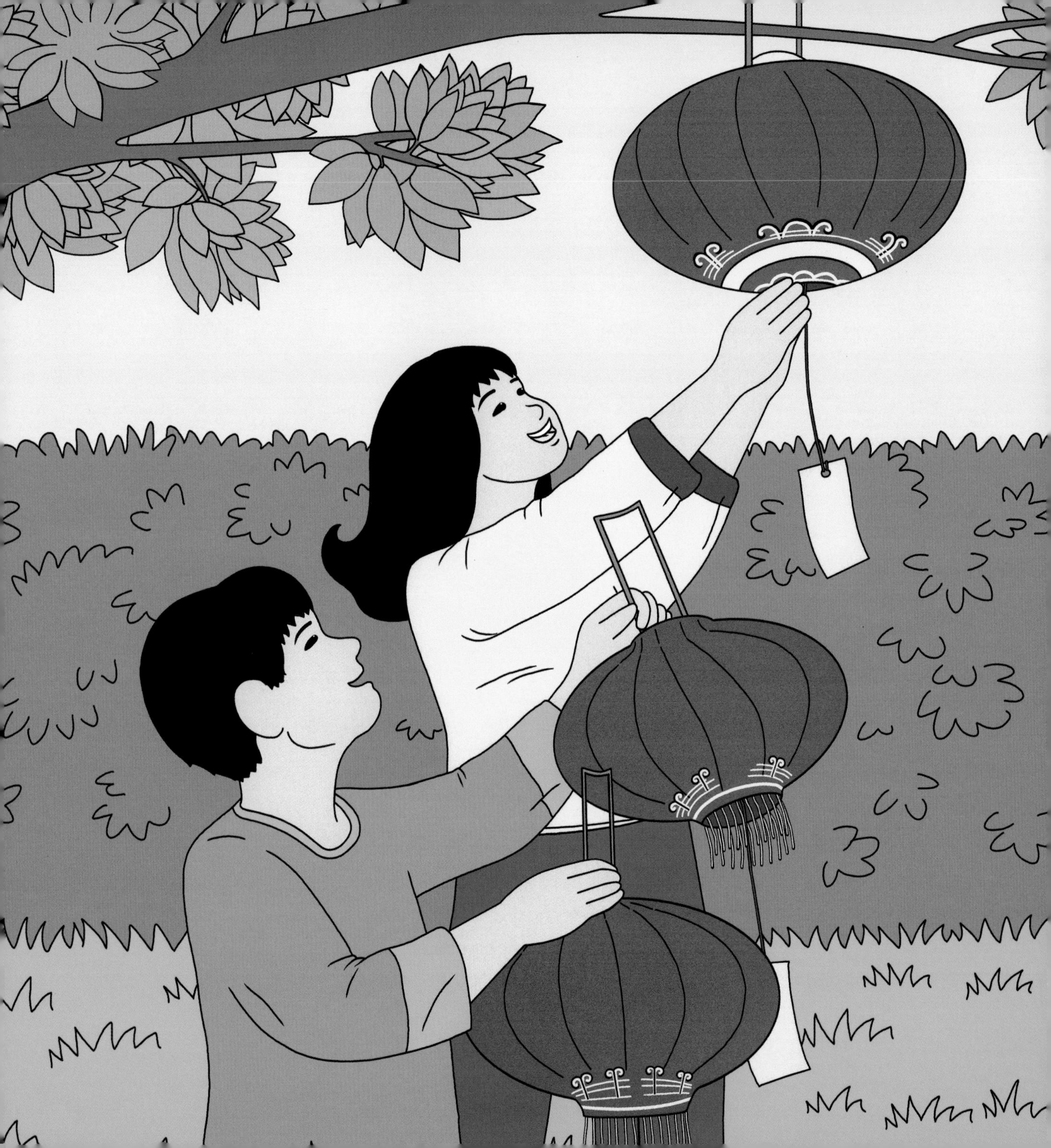

To the Chinese, the dragon
is a symbol of strength and goodness. At the
end of the parade, a team of people holding up a huge,
colorful dragon will dance down the street as a way
of wishing everyone good luck. Firecrackers
are set off throughout the holiday to
scare away evil spirits.

and watch the dragon parade pass by.

y mirar pasar el desfile del dragón.

Para los chinos, el dragón es un
símbolo de fuerza y bondad. Al terminar el desfile,
un grupo de gente cargando un dragón enorme y colorido
bailará por la calle como deseo para todos de la buena
suerte. Petardos se encienden durante la festividad
para espantar a los espíritus malignos.

Then you cover your ears
as firecrackers explode
in the sky.

Luego te cubres tus orejas
cuando los petardos
estallan en el cielo.

Chinese New Year is the oldest and most important holiday in China, and it is celebrated by Chinese people all over the world. Chinese New Year can fall anywhere between January 20 and February 19. The Chinese lunar calendar is represented by twelve animals. They are the same as the twelve Chinese zodiac animal signs. Each year is represented by one animal. Chinese believe that the animal ruling the year you were born influences your personality. As they begin the new year, the Chinese believe that they should put the past behind them. Holiday preparations that symbolize this include cleaning the house, paying off debts, buying new clothes, and getting haircuts. It is also a time for families to reunite and give thanks to their ancestors, who laid the foundation for the family's good fortune. Houses are decorated with flowers and with paper decorations that express wishes for good luck, happiness, wealth, and long life. A traditional Chinese New Year gift is a tiny red packet containing money, which is given as a symbol of good luck. Both the lion dance and the dragon dance are performed at many Chinese New Year's festivals. Lions are considered to be good omens and the dragon dance is thought to bring good luck in the coming year. Setting off firecrackers is a holiday activity believed to drive away evil spirits.

El Año Nuevo Chino es el día festivo más viejo y más importante de la China, y se celebra por la gente de la China por todo el mundo. El Año Nuevo Chino puede caer en cualquier día de entre del 20 de enero hasta el 19 de febrero. El calendario chino lunar se representa por doce animales. Son los mismos que los doce animales zodíacos chinos. Un animal representa cada año. Los chinos creen que el animal que domina el año en el cual uno nace influye la personalidad. Cuando comienzan el año nuevo, los chinos creen que deben dejar lo pasado en el pasado. Las preparaciones para este día festivo que simbolizan esto, incluyen, limpiar casa, pagar las deudas, comprar ropa nueva, y cortarse el pelo. También es un tiempo de reunirse con familia y dar gracias por los antepasados, quienes formaron la fundación para la buena fortuna de la familia. Las casas se decoran con flores y con decoraciones de papel que expresan los deseos de la buena suerte, felicidad, riqueza, y una vida extensa. Un regalo tradicional para el Año Nuevo Chino es un pequeño paquete rojo que contiene dinero, que se regala como símbolo de la buena suerte. Ambos bailes del león y del dragón se desempeñan en muchos festivales del Año Nuevo Chino. Los leones se consideran como buenos agüeros y el baile del dragón se cree, trae la buena suerte para el año entrante. Encender

DID YOU KNOW...

Use the Holiday Happenings series to expose children to the world around them.

- Some Chinese believe that if you cry on New Year's Day, you will cry all through the year. That is why children are not punished or spanked on that day, even if they are mischievous.
- Chinese people believe it is a lucky sign to hear songbirds or see red-colored birds on Chinese New Year.
- The Chinese lunar calendar is represented by twelve animals, with each year represented by one animal. The animals are: the rat, ox, tiger, rabbit, dragon, snake, horse, ram, monkey, rooster, dog, and pig.
- Old people in China often forget their age because most people just remember that they were born in the Year of the Monkey, Rooster, etc.
- Decorations for Chinese New Year are often colored red. To Chinese people the color red represents happiness and also symbolizes fire, which, according to legend, can drive away bad luck.

BUILDING CHARACTER...

Use the Holiday Happenings series to help instill positive character traits in your children.
This Chinese New Year emphasize self-confidence.

- Why is it important to have self-confidence?
- What are you really good at?
- What do you consider to be your special talent?
- When you doubt yourself, how can you remember what's special about you?

CULTURE CONNECTION...

Use the Holiday Happenings series to expand children's view of other cultures.

- Find out which countries celebrate Chinese New Year.
- How do people in other countries celebrate Chinese New Year?
- Are these celebrations similar to the way people in your country celebrate Chinese New Year?

TRY SOMETHING NEW... Begin a scrapbook about you! Include pictures of yourself playing
sports, celebrating your birthday, and just having fun. Look at it at the beginning of the year. Seeing all of your accomplishments will remind you of how special you are!

For more information on the Holiday Happenings series or to find activities
that coordinate with it, explore our website at **www.dingles.com**.

Chinese New Year Lanterns

Goal: To decorate for Chinese New Year using lanterns

Craft: Colorful lanterns

Materials: Colored construction paper, a ruler, a pencil, scissors, either glue, tape, or a stapler

Directions:

1. Turn a piece of construction paper so the long side faces you. Fold the paper in half so it becomes a thin rectangle.

2. Using the ruler, measure down 1 inch from the top of the paper and draw a light line across the paper on the 1-inch marks.

3. Using the scissors, cut from the fold line straight upward, stopping at the 1-inch line at the top of the paper.

4. Repeat step 3 across the entire length of the paper. Space your cuts from ½ inch to 1 inch apart.

5. Carefully unfold the paper, keeping it horizontal.

6. Bend the two short sides of the paper so they meet and overlap.

7. Either glue, tape, or staple the two short edges together at the top and bottom of the lantern.

8. Use the ruler and pencil to measure a strip of paper that is 6 inches long and ½ inch wide. Then cut it out.

9. Either glue, tape, or staple one side of the strip of paper to the top of the lantern. Then bend the strip to form a handle and attach it to the lantern top.

10. If you really want to be festive, make several lanterns of different colors and string them along a piece of twine or yarn. Put a piece of tape on the handle of each one to keep them all in place.

Judy Zocchi

is the author of the Global Adventures, Holiday Happenings, Click & Squeak's Computer Basics, and Paulie and Sasha series. She is a writer and lyricist who holds a bachelor's degree in fine arts/theater from Mount Saint Mary's College and a master's degree in educational theater from New York University. She lives in Manasquan, New Jersey, with her husband, David.

Rebecca Wallis

was born in Cornwall, England, and has a bachelor's degree in illustration from Falmouth College of Arts. She has illustrated a wide variety of books for children, and she divides her time between Cornwall and London.